Basics

chain stitch (ch)

1 Make a loop in the thread, crossing the ball end over the tail. Put the hook through the loop, yarn over the hook, and draw it through the first loop.
2 Yarn over the hook and draw through the loop. Repeat for the desired number of chain stitches.

beaded chain stitch (bcs)

Slide a bead against the base of the loop on the hook. Work a chain stitch. The bead is between the chains.

single crochet (sc)

1 Insert the hook through the front and back of the first or second stitch from the hook. Yarn over and draw through the chain (two loops remain on the hook).
2 Yarn over and draw through both loops (one loop remains on the hook).

slip stitch (sl)

Go into the next stitch as for a single crochet. Yarn over, and draw through the stitch and the loop.

double crochet (dc)

1 Yarn over. Insert the hook through the second stitch from the hook, yarn over, and draw through the stitch (three loops remain on the hook).
2 Yarn over and draw through two loops on the hook (two loops remain on the hook).
3 Yarn over and draw through the remaining two loops on the hook (one loop remains on the hook).

beaded double crochet (bdc)

1 Yarn over. Insert the hook through the second stitch from the hook, yarn over, and draw through the stitch (three loops remain on the hook).
2 Slide a bead against the base of the

remaining two loops on the hook (one loop remains on the hook).

treble crochet (tr)

1 Yarn over twice. Insert the hook through the second or third stitch from the hook, yarn over, and draw through the stitch (four loops remain on the hook).
2 Yarn over and draw through two loops (three loops remain on the hook).

Basics

3 Yarn over and draw through two loops (two loops remain on the hook).
4 Yarn over and draw through both loops (one loop remains on the hook).

join a ring

1 A slip stitch is used to join the first and last chains to form a ring. Insert the hook into the first stitch, going under the top part of the chain in the front and under the back loop.
2 Yarn over, and bring the yarn through both the stitch and the loop on the hook.

lark's head knot

Fold a cord in half and lay it behind a ring, loop, bar, etc. with the fold pointing down. Bring the ends through the ring from back to front and through the fold. Tighten.

surgeon's knot

Cross the right end over the left and go through the loop. Go through the loop again. Pull ends to tighten. Cross the left end over the right and go through once. Tighten.

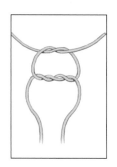

tubular peyote

1 String an even number of beads to equal the desired circumference. Tie in a circle, leaving some ease.
2 Even-numbered beads form row 1 and odd numbered beads, row 2. (Numbers indicate rows.) Put the ring over a form if desired. Go through the first bead to the left of the knot. Pick up a bead (#1 of row 3), skip a bead, and go through the next bead. Repeat around until you're back to the start.

 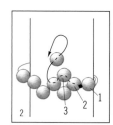

3 Since you started with an even number of beads, you need to work a "step up" to be in position for the next row. Go through the first beads on rows 2 and 3. Pick up a bead and go through the second bead of row 3; continue. (If you begin with an odd number of beads, there won't be a step up; you'll keep spiraling.)

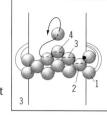

loops: opening

1 Hold the jump ring with two pairs of chainnose pliers or chainnose and roundnose pliers, as shown.
2 To open the jump ring, bring the tips of one pair of pliers toward you and push the tips of the other pair away.

3 The jump ring is open. Reverse the steps to close.

wrapped loops

1 Make sure you have at least 1¼ in. (3.2cm) of wire above the bead. With the tip of your chainnose pliers, grasp the wire directly above the bead. Bend the wire (above the pliers) into a right angle.
2 Using roundnose pliers, position the jaws vertically in the bend.

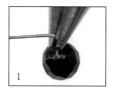 

3 Bring the wire over the top jaw of the roundnose pliers.
4 Keep the jaws vertical and reposition the pliers' lower jaw snugly into the loop. Curve the wire downward around the bottom of the roundnose pliers. This is the first half of a wrapped loop.

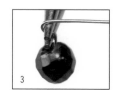 

5 Position the chainnose pliers' jaws across the loop.
6 Wrap the wire around the wire stem, covering the stem between the loop and the top bead. Trim the excess wire and press the cut end close to the wraps with chainnose pliers.

Retro bracelets

R etro-style bracelets experience an upswing in popularity every few years—be ready for the next one with one of these sturdy bracelets. It's easy to make one: simply crochet a band (or use wide elastic if you wish) for the base and stitch on an array of your favorite buttons.

The black glass buttons in the bracelets above date from the 1870s to the 1960s. Other possibilities include Bakelite buttons, metal picture buttons, cut steel buttons, and buttons with shell and sea creature motifs. The choices are as varied as your imagination and your button cache. See "Basics," p. 3, for crochet instructions.

1 Chain stitch a 1-1¼-in. (2.5-3cm) base row (approximately seven to eight stitches).
2 Work back across the row in single crochet (sc), ch1, and turn. Repeat until the band fits comfortably around your wrist. Ch1 and turn.
3 To make the clasp's loop end, sc in the first two stitches and chain eight. Then, sc in the last two stitches to connect the loop. Cut the thread and pull the tail through the last loop.

When you sew on the buttons, cover the exposed tails.
4 To keep the bracelet from stretching, use sewing thread to stitch along the length of the bracelet, approximately ¼ in. (6mm) from the edges. Make several backstitches to secure the thread as you sew.
5 Lay out the buttons you want to sew onto the bracelet. Consider choosing a dramatic button for a centerpiece and working from the center to each end. Cover the entire crocheted base, fitting the buttons together like pieces of a puzzle. Use an oblong or round button for the clasp.
6 As you sew the buttons on, stitch through more than one crochet thread to anchor each button. Buttons with wire shanks tend to sink into the crochet stitches; those with wide or flat shanks rest against the soft surface. ●
– *Sadie Jackman*

materials

- skein medium-weight crochet cotton
- crochet hook, size F (or to match yarn size)
- **24-36** buttons, assorted sizes, shapes, colors
- sewing thread
- needles

Ribbon yarn belt

This fun and fashionable crochet belt, which can also be worn as a scarf, works up quickly with one or two skeins of ribbon yarn. Select lightweight beads, particularly if you plan to wear it as a scarf.

The simple pattern sequence is six rows of single crochet (sc) and one row of double crochet (dc), chain (ch) one, and double crochet across (see "Basics," p. 3, for all stitches). The chain one space leaves room for the beads to be sewn on the belt when it is complete. The fringe consists of two 36-in. (.9m) chains that are attached to the donut pendant with a lark's head knot (see "Basics"); the finished sash is composed of four 18-in. (45.7cm) chains with beads at each end.

Gauge for this project is single crochet: 7 stitches (sts), 6 rows = 2 in. (5cm) and double crochet: ch 1, dc: 7 sts, 1 row = ½ in. (1.2cm). Take time to check your gauge, and switch your crochet hook size if needed.

❶ **Row 1:** Ch2. 2sc in second chain from hook, ch1. Turn.
Row 2: Sc in first sc, 2sc in next sc, ch1. Turn. (3sc total.)
Row 3: Sc twice in first sc, sc in second sc, sc twice in last sc, ch1. Turn. (5sc total.)
Row 4: Sc in first sc, sc across, ch1, turn.
Row 5: Sc twice in first sc, sc across, Sc twice in last sc, ch 1. Turn. (7sc total.)
Row 6: Sc in first sc, sc across, ch1, turn.
Rows 7-11: Sc in first sc, sc across, ch1, turn.
Row 12: Repeat row 11, ch2, turn.
Row 13: Dc in first sc, * ch1 skip next sc, dc in next sc. Repeat from * twice, ch1, turn.
Row 14: Sc in first dc, *sc in ch1 space, sc in next dc. Repeat from * twice, ch1, turn.

Rows 15-18: Sc in first sc, sc across, ch1, turn.
Row 19: Repeat row 18, ch 2, turn.
Row 20: Repeat row 13.
❷ Repeat Rows 14-20 until you are 3 in. (7.6cm) from the desired length.
❸ At 3 in. from the desired length, taper the end as follows:
Rows 1-6: Sc in first sc, sc across, sc in last sc, ch1. Turn. (7sc total.)
Row 7: Skip first sc, sc in next sc, sc in the next 3 sc, skip sc, sc in last sc, ch1. Turn. (5sc total.)
Row 8: Sc in first sc, sc across, ch1, turn.
Row 9: Skip first sc, sc in next sc, skip sc, sc in last sc, ch1. Turn (3sc total.)
Row 10: Sc in first sc, sc across, ch 1, turn.
Row 11: Skip first sc, sc in next sc.
❹ Fasten off. Weave the tail at each end of belt into back.

adding beads

❶ Attach the donut pendant by pulling ¾ in. (2cm) of the belt end through the donut pendant. Wrap over the pendant and stitch to the back of the belt with a sewing needle and thread (**photo a**). Repeat at the opposite end of the belt.
❷ To make the fringe chains, ch160 or 36 in. Make four fringe chains, two for each donut pendant.
❸ Attach two fringe chains to each donut pendant using lark's head knots.
❹ Thread a round bead and oblong bead at the end of each rope. Tie a knot below the oblong bead, leaving a 1-in. (2.5cm) tail (**photo b**).
❺ Thread the sewing needle with Nymo and sew beads in the spaces between the double crochets (three beads per row; **photo c**). ❍
— *Sharon Mann*

a

b

c

materials
- skein ribbon yarn (for size small belt; use **2** skeins for medium or large belt)
- crochet hook, size I/9, or size needed to obtain gauge
- **2** 40mm stone donut pendants
- approximately **50** lightweight large-hole beads
- Nymo D beading thread to match yarn
- sewing needle

Tools: scissors

Silk & stone bag

An attractive cabochon bezeled by silk sewing thread worked in single and treble crochet makes a great centerpiece for this bag. Weave a five-bead picot around the sides and bottom and string fringe from the picot. Hang the bag from beaded-chain links. See "Basics," p. 3, for crochet stitches.

front

Use double strands of thread throughout. Work in the back loops of a stitch unless otherwise instructed. Start with the main color (A) thread. Ch 16 and join with a sl st to form a ring. End all rows with sl st in beg st. Join all new colors of thread (begin the stitch with the old color, and finish the stitch in the new color) in any corner.

Rnd 1: (Sc in nx 3 st, 3 sc in nx st) 4x, end with sl st in beg st (24 st in all).

Rnd 2: (Sc in nx 5 st, 3 sc in nx st) 4x (32 st in all).

Rnd 3: (Sc in nx 7 st, 3 sc in nx st) 4x (40 st in all).

Rnd 4: (Sc in nx 9 st, 3 sc in nx st) 4x (48 st in all).

Rnd 5: (Sc in nx 11 st, 3 sc in nx st) 4x (56 st in all).

Rnd 6: (Sc in nx 13 st, 3 sc in nx st) 4x (64 st in all).

Rnds 1-6 form the backing for the cabochon. The cab rests inside the crocheted bezel. If your cab is larger than the one shown here, work additional rows in the pattern.

Rnd 7-8: Sc in each st around and end with a sl st in the beg st. If two rnds do not reach up the side of the cab, repeat this step until the sides are even with the face of the cab, and it fits snugly.

Rnd 9: Working in the front loops of Rnd 6 on the bezel side of the fabric, join in any corner. Sc in nx st and in each st to the corner, work 3 sc in corner st and continue around in pattern.

Rnd 10: Working in the back loops only, sc in each st to the corner and sc 3 st in each corner st.

Rnd 11: Repeat Rnd 10 with B-color thread.

Rnd 12: Join C-color thread and work spike stitches. *Sc in nx st, sc around Rnd 11 into Rnd 10 (**see photo a,** p. 10) to corner, 3 sc in corner st.* Repeat from * to * 3x.

Rnd 13: Join D-color thread and repeat Rnd 10.

Rnd 14: Join A-color thread and repeat Rnd 10.

Rnd 15: Join E-color thread and repeat Rnd 10.

Rnd 16: Join B-color thread. *Sc in nx st, sc around Rnd 15 into Rnd 14 to corner. Three sc in corner st. Space the Xs by working out the stitch count so that the four Xs line up under the cab (this will vary depending on whether you added rows for the cab after Rnd 6). To crochet an X (**see photo a**), *work a tr in the front loop of Rnd 12. Three sts ahead, sk one st in Rnd 15 and sc in nx 2 sts on Rnd 15. Work a tr in the front loop of Rnd 12, 3 sts back from the last tr. Sk one st on Rnd 15, sc in nx 2 st on Rnd 15.* Repeat from * to * once more.

Rnd 17: Join C in corner just passed. *Sc in nx st, sc spike into Rnd 15 to corner. Three sc in corner st. Sc in each st across, spike into Rnd 15 just before and just after the Xs. Three sc in corner.* Repeat from * to * once.

Rnd 18-20: Join A-color thread and repeat Rnd 10.

Rnd 21: Join E-color thread and repeat Rnd 10.

Rnd 22: Join C-color thread. Spike every

abbreviations

beg beginning	**sl st** slip stitch
ch chain	**st** stitch
nx next	**sts** stitches
rnd round/row	**tr** treble crochet
sc single crochet	**x** times
sk skip	

materials

- 16 x 16mm cabochon
- **65** 4mm faceted beads
- **25** 4mm cube beads
- **24** 4mm round beads, one or two colors
- **48** 4mm flat daisy spacers
- **48** 3mm smooth-edged spacers
- Japanese cylinder beads
  8g main color
  1g each of two accent colors
- silk sewing thread, Gütermann or Tire brand, main color (A) and six accent colors (B-F)
- steel crochet hook, size 14
- beading needles, #12
- Nymo D beading thread to match main color
- Thread Heaven
- 2 yd. (1.8m) 24- or 26-gauge wire
- 2 in. (5cm) chain
- hook-and-eye clasp
- 2 3-4mm jump rings
- epoxy glue

Tools: chainnose and roundnose pliers, diagonal wire cutters

Rnd 16 treble crochet Xs

Rnd 12 spike stitches

a

b

c

d

☐ main color (MC)
◼ accent color A
◼ accent color B

⬡ 4mm round

◼ 4mm cube

figure 1

figure 2

figure 3

other st around Rnd 21 into Rnd 20.
Rnd 23: Repeat Rnd 10.

back

❶ For the back of the bag, use A-color thread and work as for the front through Rnd 6. For Rnds 7-23, repeat Rnd 10. Add extra rnds if you did on the front.

❷ With right sides facing out, whipstitch the sides and bottom of the front and back together using A-color thread.

picot and fringe

Space 13 strands of fringe along the sides and 15 strands along the bottom. If you added extra rnds to the body of the bag, you may want to add more fringe.

❶ Thread a needle with 3-4 ft. (.9-1.2m) of Nymo. Sew into the top edge of the bag and tie off the end inside the bag.

❷ Sewing through both pieces of fabric, go through the second stitch from the top corner, then go from front to back through the third stitch. Pick up two main color (MC) cylinder beads, one accent color-A cylinder, and two MCs. Skip a stitch and sew from front to back through the next stitch (**figure 1**).

❸ Repeat step 2 around the bottom and second side of the bag. As you work the second side, sew from back to front. Turn the piece when finished.

❹ Go back through the last three beads strung and, exiting the A, follow the stringing sequence and thread path in **figure 2**. Repeat 12 more times.

❺ As you exit the A to turn the corner, make one fringe following the stringing sequence in **figure 3**.

❻ Fringes 2-3: For each of the nx two strands, add four MCs to each side of the first MC section, and two MCs to each side of the second MC section.

Fringes 4-8: For each of the nx five strands, add four MCs to each side of the first MC section, and four MCs to each side of the second MC section.

To add fringe to the second half, reverse the stringing pattern and delete the MCs added in each row.

cabochon

Apply glue to the inside of the bezel fabric. Gently slide the cab into the bezel and allow the glue to dry.

chain

The wrapped-loop components measure from ½-¾ in. (1.3-1.9cm). Each side of the chain is 10 in. (25cm), excluding the clasp ends. Add or eliminate components to adjust the length. Three versions of the component repeat along the chain.

❶ Cut a 3-in. (7.6cm) piece of wire. Begin a wrapped loop at one end (see "Basics"). Slide the hook clasp into the loop and finish the wrap.

❷ Slide on a spacer, a 3mm round, and a spacer. Make a second wrapped loop in the same plane as the first (**photo b**).

❸ Cut a 3-in. piece of wire, start a wrapped loop, and slide the loop through the end loop of the component made in step 1 (**photo c**). Finish the wraps. Then repeat step 2.

❹ Repeat step 3, varying the components as shown in **photo d** for one side of the chain. Slide a 3-4mm jump ring in the last loop of the chain.

❺ Repeat steps 1-4 to make a second chain, adding the other half of the clasp as in step 1.

❻ Open the jump ring (see "Basics") on one end of a chain and slide it through both pieces of fabric near a top corner of the bag. Close the ring. Repeat on the other side of the bag. ●
– *Melody MacDuffee*

Patterned lariat

Whether you're looking for a challenging or simple bead crochet project, this lariat offers enough options to suit a range of interests. The version shown here consists of nine patterned sections of bead crochet connected with art glass beads, a peyote-stitch toggle, and bead caps worked in herringbone. To simplify the lariat, work with fewer colors, make fewer but longer sections, and buy the toggle and bead caps. See "Basics," p. 3, for crochet instructions.

crocheted tubes

❶ Use a Big Eye needle to string 3-5 ft. (.9-1.5m) of beads onto the yarn. (To match the bead and color sequence in this lariat, refer to the sidebar on p. 12.)

❷ Leaving an 8-in. (20cm) tail, work eight bead chain stitches (bcs). Connect the chain into a circle with a slip stitch.

❸ Work in bead slip-stitch (**figure 1,** p. 13) until the tube is 4 in. (10cm) long if you plan to make a color change (see sidebar), or about 5½ in. (14cm) without a change.

4 Crochet a total of nine tubes.

5 Block the tubes to prevent them from stretching: Pin one end to a terry cloth towel, pull slightly, and pin the other end. Dampen the tubes with water and let them dry overnight.

bead connections

1 Line up your tubes in the correct color sequence. Thread one tapestry needle on the tail of the first tube and a second needle on the tail of another. Cross the needles through an 8mm bead (**photo a**).

2 Working with either needle, go through one bead on the end row of the tube, then go through a bead a few stitches away. (They should be opposite each other.) Go back through the 8mm bead (**photo b**). Repeat with the other needle to connect the second tube. Tighten the yarn so the tubes press up against the 8mm bead (**photo c**).

3 Repeat twice, going through different beads each time.

4 Repeat to connect the remaining tubes into a continuous rope.

toggle

1 Center a needle on 2 yd. (1.8m) of Silamide and work with doubled thread. Pick up 12 cylinder beads and go through them again to form a ring. Slip the ring onto a knitting needle or other cylinder.

2 Work in tubular peyote (see "Basics") until the toggle is about the same length as the donut's outer diameter. Keep the tension very tight. Secure both tails in the stitches and trim.

3 Thread the needle with 1 yd. (.9m) of Silamide, pick up a 6º bead, and go through it again in the same direction. Sew through the peyote tube, lodging the 6º bead in the tube's center.

4 String a bicone and a 15º seed bead. Turn, and go back through the bicone and the tube (**photo d**). Repeat on the other end of the tube.

5 Sew through the bicones and toggle several times to anchor the beads to the ends of the toggle. Secure the tails in the stitches and trim.

bead caps

1 Thread a needle with 2½-3 yd. (2.3-2.7m) of Silamide or Nymo D.

a

c

b

d

patterns

Each tube in this lariat is worked in the following pattern: eight 11ºs in color A followed by an eight-bead alternating pattern of 11ºs in A and 8ºs in any color. To follow this design, change colors about 1½ in. (4cm) from the tube's end and finish using the new colors. Start the next tube using the color sequence from the end of the previous tube. Before sewing the tubes together, line them up in the correct color sequence.

changing colors

To make a color change, slide the beads away from the stitches and cut the yarn, leaving a 6-in. (15cm) tail. Make one more chain stitch (no bead) and pull the tail through the loop on the hook to tie off the thread. Slide any beads that remain on the ball of yarn away from the cut end and string the next bead sequence.

To join the new yarn, insert the hook under the last bead added. Fold the new yarn about 3 in. (7.6cm) from the cut end. Grab the new yarn at the fold and pull the loop through to the inside of the crochet tube. Make a chain stitch (no bead), catching the yarn's working end and cut end. Pull the cut end until it comes loose. You will have two loose ends in the center of the tube. Work a few rows to make sure the new pattern is correct, then use a surgeon's knot (see "Basics") to tie the two ends tightly together inside the tube. Trim the ends about ¾ in. (2cm) from the knot. Continue in bead slip-stitch until the tube is the desired length.

Adjust the ends so one side is 8 in. shorter than the other.

2 Pick up eight 15ºs and slide them to 6 in. (15cm) from the end of the longer thread. Go through the beads again to form a ring. Tighten the thread and maintain a tight tension (**figure 2, a-b**).

Row 1: Begin working in herringbone. Pick up two beads and go through the next two beads. Repeat, picking up four pairs of beads in this row (**b-c**).

Row 2: Align the threads so the shorter one extends about an inch (2.5cm)

below the last bead you've gone through. (From this point, you'll be working with doubled thread.) Go through the first bead added in the previous row, pick up two beads, and go through the second bead of the pair (**c-d**). Pick up one bead and go through the first bead of the next pair. Repeat until you've picked up the last single bead (**d-e**).

Row 3: To step up and start the row, go through the first bead in rows 1 and 2 (**e-f**). Work as in row 2, but add two

materials

54-in. (1.4m) necklace

- 30mm diameter donut (art glass donut by Kathy Perras/Itzart, www.kathyperras.com)
- **8** 8mm art glass beads (Kathy Perras)
- seed beads
  60g size 8º, one or more colors
  40g size 11º, one or more colors
  2g size 15º, one or two colors
- 2g Japanese cylinder beads
- **2** 5 or 6mm bicone crystals
- ball of #20 or 30 wt. crochet cotton or perle cotton, #8
- crochet hook, size 8-10 (to match yarn choice)
- Silamide or Nymo D (if not using 30 wt. cotton)
- beeswax to condition Nymo
- eye pin
- **3** 6.5mm split rings
- Big Eye needle
- **2** thin tapestry needles
- beading needles, #10 or 12
- knitting needle, size 5, or other thin cylinder

Tools: roundnose pliers, chainnose pliers, wire cutters

e

g

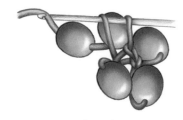

f

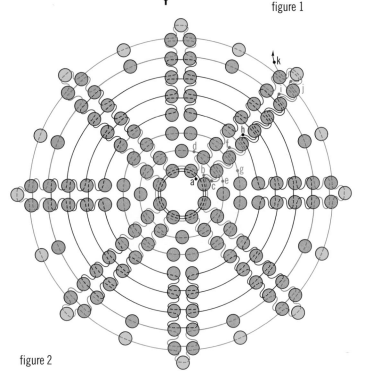

figure 1

figure 2

beads between each pair instead of one (**f-g**).

Rows 4-6: Step up to start each row as before (**g-h**). Pick up two beads and go through the next bead. Go through the first bead of the new pair added in the previous row, pick up two beads, and go through the next bead. Continue around the circle. The bead cap will begin to take on its cup shape in the sixth round (**h-i**).

Row 7: Repeat Row 6, but pick up one bead between each pair of beads (**i-j**).

Row 8: Pick up one bead instead of two and go back through the second bead of the pair. Pick up one bead and go through the next bead. Repeat around the circle (**j-k**). Reinforce the bead cap by sewing up and down each stack of beads. Weave in and trim the tails.

❸ Make a second bead cap.

finishing

❶ Working on either end of the rope, weave the remaining tail into the tube. Thread a beading needle with 2 yd. (1.8m) of crochet cotton (if using #30) or Silamide and anchor it in the tube.

String a bead cap, an 8º seed bead, and enough 11ºs to circle the edge of your donut. Go back through the 8º and the bead cap, tighten the thread, and secure it in the tube (**photo e**).

❷ Go back through the bead cap and 8º, string another loop of 11ºs around the donut, and go back through the 8º and bead cap. Secure the thread. Reinforce the loops by making at least one more pass through these beads.

❸ To finish the other end, thread a tapestry needle on the tube's tail. Sew through the eye of the eye pin to secure

it in the tube. Trim the tail.

❹ Thread a bead cap and several 8ºs onto the wire. Make a wrapped loop (see "Basics") next to the end bead (**photo f**).

❺ Make a short chain using one or more split rings and attach them to the loop. Make sure the length of the toggle connection is at least half the length of the toggle bar.

❻ Stitch the end split ring securely to the center of the toggle (**photo g**). ●

– Linda Lehman

Crocheted wire bezels

Create beautiful lacy silver frames for stones, cabochons, and found objects—all you need is some fine-gauge wire and a steel crochet hook! Crochet the front of the silver frame first. Then crochet the back and join the two pieces with slip stitch. Before completing the join, slip the cabochon into the bezel. It must fit very tightly. Finish by adding a purchased or shaped wire bail for hanging. If you wish, you can also crochet loops of beads around the edge of the frame. String the pendant on a purchased chain or a necklace of beads. For your first pendant, you might want to start with craft wire, which will help you adjust to the feel of crocheting with wire. See "Basics," p. 3, for crochet instructions.

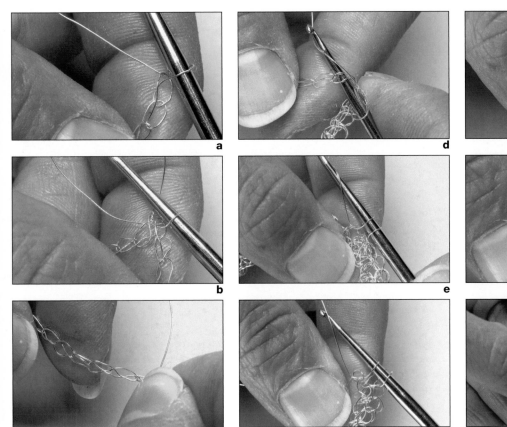

a

b

c

d

e

f

g

h

i

crocheting the front frame

Use a 40 x 30mm cabochon and work directly from the spool of wire. If your crochet is tighter or looser, or your cabochon is a different size, you will need to adjust the number of stitches.

1 Chain (ch) 36. Shape each stitch halfway up the shank of the crochet hook (**photo a**).

2 Join the chain into a ring with a slip stitch, making sure the chain is not twisted. The single-wire side of each stitch will face toward the inside of the frame (**photo b**). These loops will form a lacy edge that frames the stone.

3 Pinch and stretch this circular piece flat before continuing (**photo c**).

4 Ch1, then single crochet (sc) in the back (2-wire side) of each stitch around (**photo d**). Continue shaping each stitch halfway up the shank of the hook and pinch each stitch as you go. Join the last stitch to the first with a slip stitch.

5 Ch1 and sc one more row as in step 4 (**photo e**). Cut off the wire, leaving a 2-3-in. (5-7.6cm) tail. Pinch and stretch the frame again to make all the edges even. For a snug fit, the last row should just reach to the outer edge of the stone.

crocheting the back

1 Ch6. Shape all the stitches as described in step 1, above.

2 Ch1 and sc in the fifth chain from the start and in each of the chain stitches back to the first. Make a second sc in the first stitch (**photo f**).

3 Sc in each of the starting chain stitches again on the side opposite the first sc row (**photo g**). Put 2 scs in the last chain stitch to make the piece lie flat. Then join to the first sc in step 2 with a slip stitch (**photo h**).

4 Ch1 and sc around, shaping the stitches halfway up the hook and pinching and stretching as you go.

5 Work a total of five to six rounds of sc, or as many as you need to make the piece slightly smaller than the back of the cabochon (**photo i**).

6 Pinch and stretch again and pull the piece into an oblong shape to fit the cabochon. Do not end or cut the wire.

joining the back and front

1 Lay the frame piece on top of the back and begin to slip stitch them together at the top of the bezel (**photo j**, p. 16).

2 The outer edge of the frame is usually larger than the circumference of the back piece because it has more stitches. Decrease here and there to adjust by skipping one of the stitches on the frame. Leave about 1½ in. (3.8cm) unjoined, but do not cut the wire.

3 Now push the stone through the opening. The piece will need to be very tight, and the stone difficult to push

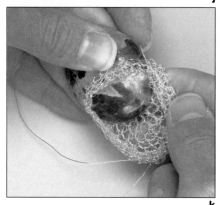

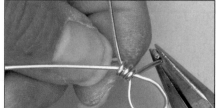

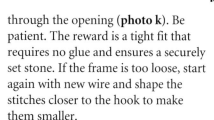

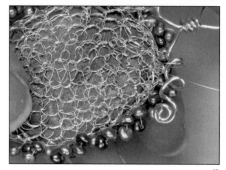

materials

- **200** small beads, 2-4mm: chips, nuggets, sterling or gold-filled, bone, shell, glass seed beads, freshwater pearls
- 40 x 30mm cabochon
- 15-20 ft. (4.6-6m) 30-gauge fine silver wire (Rio Grande)
- steel crochet hook, size 6 or 7
- purchased bail or 6mm split ring; or make your own bail with 16 in. (41cm) round or half-round 18-gauge sterling silver wire (experiment with copper wire first)

Tools: roundnose and chainnose pliers, wire cutters

through the opening (**photo k**). Be patient. The reward is a tight fit that requires no glue and ensures a securely set stone. If the frame is too loose, start again with new wire and shape the stitches closer to the hook to make them smaller.

❹ When the stone is properly seated, finish slip-stitching the pieces together. Cut the wire, leaving a 3-in. (7.6cm) tail for sewing on the bail or a 12-14-in. (31-36cm) tail for adding loops of beads. Pull the tail through the last stitch to end the crochet.

finishing

❶ If desired, string one to three small beads at a time and whipstitch the wire through the slip stitches that join the bezel pieces (**photo l**). Add beads around the entire frame.

❷ If enough wire remains, work it to the top of the pendant and use it to attach a purchased bail or a split ring set at a right angle to the pendant.

❸ If you decide to make your own 18-gauge wire bail, experiment with copper wire until you have a shape that you like. I made a large loop in the center of my wire and wrapped its base two or three times with a short piece of the same wire (**photo m**). Then I bent and coiled the two ends symmetrically with roundnose pliers. (Asymmetry can also look good.) Whipstitch the bail to the top of the pendant with the 30-gauge wire at every point where the two meet (**photo n**).

crocheting hints

• The back piece can be crocheted to fit any shape of cabochon. Just stretch a circular piece in one direction for an oblong cabochon. For a square stone, crochet the back in rows.

• Always stretch and pinch the work so the frame fits tightly after joining.

• Form each stitch into a round shape by bringing it back onto the shank of the hook before completing the stitch. The wire will hold this shape.

• Relax. Try not to pull, yank, or get tense with the hook, and handle the wire gently so it doesn't kink. The wire is very strong and amazingly forgiving, but you can't rip it out and start over if you make a mistake. ◐ – *Mary Jean Leslie*

Bead and wire crochet earrings

These double-crochet medallions work up quickly and can be embellished by adding a three-bead picot edge or dangles.

Start by sliding beads directly on the wire, then work beaded double crochet stitches to make a medallion (see "Basics," p. 3, for crochet instructions). Attach a focal bead, add the dangles or picot edge, and attach an earring wire to finish. If this is your first attempt at crocheting with wire, try some test swatches to familiarize yourself with its characteristics.

foundation chain

Uniformity in stitch size is more important than stitch gauge.

❶ Without cutting the wire from the

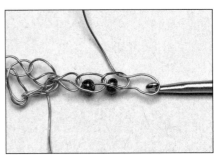

a

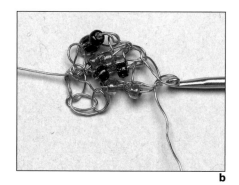
b

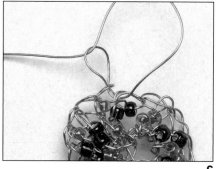
c

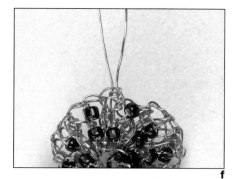
f

figure 1

g

figure 2

spool, pick up two beads in color A and two beads in color B. Pick up pairs of alternating color beads until you have strung a total of nine sets each.

❷ Leave a 5-in. (13cm) tail and make four chain stitches. Join the chain into a ring with a slip stitch.

beaded double crochet

The beads slide to the back of the piece as you work, so the back becomes the front of the finished earring.

❶ Make a beaded chain stitch (bcs). Then make a second bcs. This counts as the first double crochet (**photo a**).

❷ Work three beaded double crochet (bdc) into the first chain of the foundation ring (**photo b**).

❸ Work five bdc into the next chain.

❹ Work four bdc into the third chain.

❺ Work five bdc into the fourth chain of the foundation ring.

❻ Join the last bdc to the first bdc with

a slip stitch. Cut the wire with wire cutters and leave a 5-in. tail. Thread the tail through the slip stitch and tighten (**photo c**).

❼ Flatten the medallion if needed.

central bead

❶ Position the medallion's starting tail so it exits the beaded side.

❷ Slide on a 6mm bead (**photo d**).

❸ Thread the tail to the back, cross an existing wire, and then go to the front.

❹ Go through the 6mm again in the opposite direction (**photo e**). Thread the tail to the back of the medallion again.

loop

❶ Slide the starting tail through the stitches so it exits next to the ending tail at the edge of the medallion (**photo f**).

❷ Twist the wires together. Use roundnose pliers to form a wrapped loop (see "Basics" and **photo g**).

❸ Slide the tail through the bdc to secure it (**photo h**). Then trim it.

❹ Open the loop of an earring finding (see "Basics") and slide it through the loop at the top of the medallion. Close the loop.

❺ Make a second earring to match the first.

optional three-bead picot

❶ Cut 24 in. (61cm) of Nymo. About 6 in. (15cm) from one end, fold the cord and go through an edge loop on the medallion. Make a lark's head knot (see "Basics"). Do not trim.

❷ Thread a needle on the long end and pick up an A bead, a B bead, and an A bead. Go under the wire of the next loop and come up through the last bead added (**figure 1, a-b**).

❸ Pick up an A and a B and sew under the wire of the next loop. Then go through the last bead added (**figure 1,**